W9-ANU-560

GUINEA PIGS
AS A NEW PET

STEPHEN NELSON

CONTENTS

Photos by Dr. Herbert R. Axelrod, Isabelle Français, Michael Gilroy, H. Hansen, Ron and Val Moat, Carolyn Ruf, Brian Seed, Sally Anne Thompson, Tierfreunde Photo, and David Whiteway.

1995 Edition

Published by
T.F.H. PUBLICATIONS, INC.
1 T.F.H. Plaza
Neptune, NJ 07753
Made in the USA

Introduction

The guinea pig is a hardy little creature that can make a fine pet for people of all ages.

When the Spaniards explored and conquered much of South America during the sixteenth century, they sent back to Spain not only gold and rare parrots, but also a curious little animal that in some ways resembled a pig—and squealed like one too. This was the guinea pig or cavy, and today it is one of the world's most popular pets.

The guinea pig is undemanding in its diet, is hardy, and is a reliable breeder—though not as prolific as most other members of its order, that of the rodents. Guinea pigs come in a whole range of colors and markings and may have hair which is silky and smooth, stiff and in rosettes, or velvet-like and long. You will have plenty to choose from. These little animals will rarely bite so are very safe with children, though they are by nature nervous creatures so must be handled with much care if they are to become really tame. Another unusual characteristic of guinea pigs is that they can safely be housed with rabbits, with whom they will develop strong friendships—it is not too often that differing animals can be so kept without careful introductions but guinea pigs will not harm any creatures.

The price you will have to pay in a pet shop for a good healthy example will be very modest indeed, and even a really good show specimen will not give your bank balance a problem. Although one thinks of guinea pigs as primarily a children's pet, nothing could be further from the truth as many thousands of adults from all walks of life devote much of their free time to these little animals, which they breed and exhibit for their color or coat quality, and are judged against exacting standards laid down by the various specialist clubs that have been formed to cater to each of the many varieties. Guinea pigs can therefore be a hobby for the whole of the family as there are often special classes in cavy shows for children and also for crossbred examples which are simply kept as pets.

In their native homelands guinea pigs are still kept as pets by the various Indian tribes—as they have been since the earliest known records of the Inca civilization. The Indians do not keep their guinea pigs in cages or hutches but allow them to run freely throughout their homes and villages. They are both pets and a source of food.

In the following chapters, the text will commence by reviewing the wild guinea pigs, so you have an idea about their historical background, and it will then go on to cover every facet of keeping them as pets, for breeding, or for exhibiting, so that in whichever aspect you wish to become involved, there is complete coverage to act as a reference. The book is illustrated throughout with superb color photographs and these will do much more than words can to show you the differing varieties, but even so, brief descriptions of all the varieties are given.

Guinea pigs come in a wide array of colors and color combinations. You may have a particular choice of color in mind, which is fine, but your foremost consideration should be the selection of a healthy guinea pig.

Natural History

The scientific name of the guinea pig, or cavy as it is often called, is *Cavia aperea porcellus*, and all the domesticated forms of this animal have been developed by careful selective breeding from the wild cavies of Peru and Brazil, which have the names *Cavia aperea aperae*, *C. a. tschudii*, *C. fulgida* and *C. stolida*. It is believed that the subspecies *tschudii* is possibly the direct ancestor of our domesticated guinea pigs, though there appears to be no direct proof of this. The term "guinea" is thought to be an error for Guyana, an area in northern South America; the other theory is that the

returning Spaniards probably called at ports in Guinea on the African west coast and that people thought these little animals came from that region when the ships docked in Spain. The word *aperea* is derived from the Latin *aper*, meaning a wild boar or pig, while *porcellus* is likewise of Latin origin, meaning little pig. All scientific names of animals are of Latin or Greek origin and were first used by the Swedish naturalist Carolus Linnaeus who devised the presently used binomial system of nomenclature by which all animals are known internationally.

RODENTS

Guinea pigs are members of the highly successful animal order known as Rodentia, which contains animals as diverse as the tiny African mice which are no more than a few inches in length through the giant rodents of South America—the capybaras—which can be nearly four feet in length and

Domesticate guinea pigs are quite different from their relatives in the wild: they have rounder, plumper bodies and come in a wider variety of coat and color types.

weigh up to 54 kg (118 lbs). Although all rodents share a number of features, there is one which has not changed at all as they have diversified over the millenia and that is their gnawing front teeth, called incisors. All rodents possess two upper and two lower incisors and these grow throughout the animal's life. Behind the incisors, there is a gap, called a diastema, which in most mammals other than rodents is filled by the canine or eye teeth. Behind the diastema are the premolars and then the molars. Rodents do not crush their food like dogs or cats but grind it by lateral action after the powerful incisors have chiselled the food from its stalk.

As a point of interest, rabbits are not rodents as was commonly thought, but are contained in a related order known as Lagomorpha—their teeth differ from those of rodents in that there are eight incisors arranged in four pairs.

THE CAVY FAMILY

The order of rodents is divided into a number of suborders, one of which is

Hystricomorpha, which in turn is divided into some 16 families, one of which is Caviidae, in which are found all the guinea pigs. Guinea pigs are distributed only in South America and are found throughout most of that continent in a range of habitats from grassy lowlands to levels up to 4,500 meters in the mountains of the Andes.

All cavies have rootless molars and incisors which grow throughout the life of the animal. Some rodents have rooted molars that do not continue to grow, the hamster being one such example. The cavies have four front digits to their feet and three on the rear. Within the cavy family are found the Patagonian cavies as well as the cavies we know, the former having much longer legs, resembling a cross between a hare and a small deer.

If at first your pet shies away from you, don't be discouraged. Most guinea pigs will learn to accept and enjoy the companionship of their human family.

WILD CAVIES

The wild cavy from which the pet guinea pigs are descended is similar in shape, but its head is somewhat less massive, more resembling what would be considered a poor example by today's breeders. In the wild, cavies live in small family groups which are controlled by a single boar. They will make their homes in burrows which they will dig out or they will take over any convenient burrow vacated by another animal.

The coat of the wild cavy is nothing like that of the domesticated varieties, but is a brown agouti color which is lighter on the sides and underbelly than on the back—it is very uniform in color and markings with only very light tracings around the cheek areas and on the snout in certain examples.

Wild cavies are crepuscular feeders meaning they eat at dawn and dusk in order to avoid their many natural enemies such as hawks, owls, wild cats, snakes and other reptiles. They have little means of defending themselves so have become extremely nimble and can move at an amazing speed;

added to this they are also extremely cautious animals— a feature you will soon notice in your pets. They stay within known territories so they can quickly escape along pathways with which they are very familiar.

Although it is often stated that they cannot cope with cold weather, this is, in fact, a somewhat misleading statement made by breeders who one must assume have never visited the Andes where guinea pigs thrive. There is nothing tropical about such places on the higher slopes which can be bitterly cold at times. However, there is no doubt that domestication has softened the species up so that those strains which have been bred for generation after generation in heated breeding rooms would suffer if suddenly placed in an outdoor situation without generous consideration for their accommodation.

In the wild, guinea pigs do not drink a great deal, providing they have access to vegetable matter. The domestic varieties, however, have developed a slightly different digestive system which enables them to

contain much more food within their stomachs. In the wild, the food for guinea pigs is not easily come by and is generally of a low nutritional value. Such food is hard to digest so they have developed a digestive system not unlike that found in cows and other ruminants. Instead of regurgitating food, they expel partly digested matter in the form of soft fecal pellets which are then eaten and pass a second time through the digestive system—this is known as coprophagy. In the domestic guinea pig, you may see this happening but it is quite normal and the food pellets should not be confused with the harder fecal waste pellets. However, because domesticated varieties have high nutritional foods supplied to them, they do not exhibit this habit as much as their wild brethren.

Wild guinea pigs have much the same reproductive habits as the domestic varieties and will be discussed in the appropriate chapter on breeding. In the wild, the family unit will stay intact until one of the young boars finds itself being attacked a great deal by the senior male. At this time, it will leave the colony, undoubtedly taking one or more females with it to commence a new colony, and so the process goes on. Among the females of a colony, there is also evidence of a hierarchical system which can be seen if numerous females are kept together in a domestic environment.

Guinea pigs are a good choice for the household that is unable to accommodate a larger sized pet.

Accommodation

The type of accommodation that is required by guinea pigs will reflect whether you intend to keep just one or two or whether you plan to set up a small breeding unit. The other major factor that must be considered is whether the hutches are to be housed indoors or outdoors—this affects the relative thickness and other aspects of the materials to be used.

If the weather is pleasant, you can let your pet enjoy the great outdoors. It is essential that he be carefully supervised, lest he scamper away from you and become lost.

READY-MADE v. HOMEBUILT

There are a number of cages or hutches which are produced commercially and these vary from very poor to extremely good. The cheaper ones will be made of very thin woods and will be suitable only for indoor use, and even then will not last long. The best ones will be produced by companies that specialize in making cages, hutches, and aviaries; these are the types that you will find available in pet shops.

The alternative to buying a cage is that the handy person could make his own; this has the advantage that you could do these exactly to your own design.

Most people, however, find that it is better to purchase their guinea pig's housing from a pet shop.

THE SINGLE HUTCH

Let us consider a nice

hutch to accommodate two adult guinea pigs—a boar and sow or two sows (two boars will fight continuously so should not be housed together).

The overall size of the hutch should be about 91.5 cm (36 in) long by 38 cm (15 in) deep and 35.5 cm (14 in) high. Even if only one pet is kept (which I would never recommend as these are very social animals) then the hutch size should still be of these dimensions, which give a degree of room in which to scamper about. A variation to this is that you could make a longer hutch (and somewhat deeper) and have a dividing panel which could be removed or inserted to increase or reduce the area according to needs. Such units are more flexible as they allow young boars and sows to be separated once they reach breeding age.

If the hutch is to be kept indoors, say in a shed or outhouse, then the wood can be slightly thinner on the sides, top, and back than if kept outside, where it must be robust to withstand harsh weather. The base should be stout in any event because otherwise the urine,

cleaning, and wear and tear will quickly reduce this to the point that it rots. A good thickness for outside use would be 1.25 cm (½ in) as this will not warp if suitably treated with a good preservative to its exterior. It is also better if the wood is screwed to a wooden framework of at least 2.25 cm (1 in). It should be raised some 31 cm (12 in) above ground level on legs—which can be an extension of the frame. This not only allows air to circulate under the floor but saves you having to unduly bend down when attending to chores.

The roof of an outside hutch is better for having a slope from front to back in order that rainwater will rapidly run off; the overall roof area should be greater than that of the hutch so that there is an overhang all around, this giving the sides some measure of protection from the weather. A good roofing felt should then be placed on the roof and tacked down over and around the overhang. This hutch should last for many years providing you periodically re-paint the outside.

The inside of the hutch can be painted white or a light pastel shade of either gloss or gloss emulsion.

If thinner wood is used in construction, still fix this to a frame and double the thickness of the sides, roof, and back. Leaving a space between each, insert foam or polystyrene insulation, making the interior nice and warm in bad weather and cooler in the hot months.

The inside of the hutch should be partitioned to provide a darkened sleeping area about one third the length of the hutch. A solid door should provide access to the sleeping area from the outside so that you can clean it with ease. The guinea pigs will enter the sleeping area via an arched hole towards the front of the hutch.

The remainder of the hutch at the front should be of welded wire affixed to a wooden frame and inserted into the hutch. This can be secured by swivel catches. This can be easily removed when you want to clean the hutch out. A wire of 19 gauge is quite strong but one of a smaller number, thus thicker, is even better. Some hutches open at the front via hinged panels but I have found these less practical than the totally removable ones described. Likewise, some breeders use metal or plastic trays on the hutch floors and these are pulled out when cleaning is done. I have found these more trouble than they are worth while a good thick wood base, well-painted with a

A mother guinea pig keeping a watchful eye over her babies. This particular cavy variety is known as Dalmatian.

gloss, is very easy to clean once the front panel is removed.

A hutch used indoors need not have a sloping roof, be felt-covered, or be of the same robustness. It should, however, be painted or treated with a preservative.

BREEDING ROOMS

The prospective breeder will of course need quite a

number of hutches and these are usually built in tiers, say in blocks of nine hutches in three rows, one on top of the other. Although it would be more costly, a better design would be to have each row having a 15 cm (6 in) gap between them for air to circulate under the floors of each row. The basic design will be similar to an outside hutch but with the indicated modifications.

It should be remembered that if you plan to keep rabbits and guinea pigs together then the hutch size will need to be slightly larger to allow for the bigger size of rabbits—and considerably so, if you have one of the larger rabbit breeds.

FLOOR COVERING

The choices of floor coverings for the hutch are normally sawdust, wood shavings, or straw. Sawdust has the best absorbency but does tend to cling to fruit and greenfoods; wood shavings are better in that they do not cling to things but a deeper layer is needed because they do not soak up the urine as well; straw has the same problem and its sharper ends can sometimes create an eye problem if the guinea pig accidentally pokes itself on these.

A more recent product is shredded or granulated paper. This is harmless if eaten and has a good rate of absorption. If sawdust or wood shavings are used, then check if the wood had been chemically treated, as this type is not desirable just in case the guinea pigs ingest any which could be toxic to them. What I have found to be a good combination is to lay sheets of newspaper on the floor and then cover this lightly with sawdust, but in the bedding area only I put hay on the paper in which the guinea pigs make a nice snug bed.

FEEDING UTENSILS

The best feeder dishes are those made of ceramic or the non-tip type, made of aluminum. These can be kept clean and small. The size used for cats is just about the right height for guineas. You can easily devise simple troughs for oats which can be attached to the inside of the hutch so that your pets will not knock them over. Rabbits, however, will delight in hurling plastic dishes around the hutch, so consider this if guinea pigs share the same housing.

Open water pots can be used but these quickly become fouled with sawdust, feces, and food. The best means of supplying water is the inverted water bottle. These are clipped to the wire fronts of the cages and operate by gravity. The guinea pigs lick the ball-bearing in their metal spouts and this pushes the ball in, thus releasing water. Those with aluminum spouts are the best as they do not rust. The water should be changed daily, and during cold weather, if the guinea pigs are housed outdoors, check that the tip of the feeder does not freeze.

OUTDOOR HUTCH & RUN

During the summer months, your pets will appreciate plenty of exercise in your yard or garden and this is easily achieved by constructing a wooden framework which is made into panels that are covered with welded wire of 19 gauge. These can be bolted together to form a run. The top panels can be hinged so that you can easily pick up your pets when required, and these panels will be needed because, while guinea pigs are poor climbers, a cat might easily jump in and attack or frighten them if the

"Open water pots can be used but these quickly become fouled with sawdust, feces, and food. The best means of supplying water is the inverted water bottle."

run is not fully enclosed. If the ground is very level, then a base will not be needed and the guineas can thus graze on the lawn; however, even if you have a wire base, your pets will still be able to graze and there would be no risk of their escaping from under the edges of the pen.

One end of the pen should have a wooden floor, sides, and roof so that your pets can retreat into this to escape the heat of direct sunshine whenever they wish—this is most important or else they risk becoming too hot. Such a unit as this can easily be moved around the lawn to provide fresh grazing, and the fecal pellets expelled will be a useful manure for the lawn which will quickly grow within a couple of days to its normal height.

Although most breeders confine their activities to indoor rooms, it is possible to have a series of hutches connected to an outdoor run. This is undoubtedly a much more satisfactory method of housing as it allows the guineas plenty of fresh air and exercise. Their breeding vigor will also improve as a direct result. In such situations, it would be better to have a concrete base to the run area which will otherwise become soiled with feces.

Another possibility for just a couple of pets would be to have a small bedding hutch placed on a raised platform in an outhouse or shed. The platform is extended to form a run and the sides and top are panelled in welded wire.

Within the run can be placed various rocks and plastic tubes with which the guinea pigs can play. This makes a really interesting home for the pets because they will enjoy the extra room and things to play around, and your children can watch them even when the weather is bad. With a little imagination, you can transform your pets' housing from a restricted hutch to a very desirable residence that will be as esthetically pleasing as it is effective.

WINTERING OUTDOORS

In the previous chapter, I stated that guinea pigs can, in fact, cope with cold weather. For many years, I kept guinea pigs together with rabbits in outdoor enclosures throughout the year, and during winter the temperatures occasionally dropped to below zero for short periods. The guinea pigs had no problems coping with such weather and seemed to take great delight when it snowed. As a precaution, pregnant females were taken indoors to have their babies during the colder months, but this was as much for my own convenience of keeping an eye on them as it was for any fears that they could not cope with such harsh weather. Furthermore (and this cannot be stressed too much), their housing was made of very thick timber and during the winter they were supplied with very liberal quantities of good hay. The wire fronts to their hutches carried clip-on Plexiglas sheets for added protection from rain, and hutches were so positioned that they were in sheltered sites to avoid driving rain or winds.

Only if you are prepared to invest a reasonable amount of cash into quality accommodation should you consider keeping guinea pigs outdoors if you live in northern climates.

Outdoor exercise is good for your pet and he will most likely enjoy it, but be sure he is protected from dogs, cats, and other animals who may injure or frighten him.

CLEANING

Hutches should be cleaned each week, or more often if necessary. Pay particular attention to the corners where parasites can hide. One corner will tend to be used as a toilet so place extra sawdust in this once the site is established. An occasional anti-mite spraying of the hutch will be beneficial. If you plan to breed, it always pays to have one or two spare hutches so you can really give them a thorough cleaning and leave them empty for a while on a rotational basis. Food dishes and water containers should be cleaned daily.

STOCKROOM EXTRAS

In the breeder's stockroom, there are a number of items and services that will be found useful. Obviously, an electric supply will be useful so that one can do many chores in the evenings after work when it is dark in the autumn and winter months. Do not have excessive heat but just sufficient to take the chill from the air—more for your own comfort than for any need on the part of your stock. A water supply and drainage facilities to the stockroom is a real advantage, but do not overlook necessary local planning permissions.

One very useful extra would be an ionizer which simply fits into a light socket. These are inexpensive to purchase and very economic to run. What they do is to release negative ions which cling to dust and microscopic bacteria to render them harmless; they are deposited on the paintwork and ionizer unit where they can easily be wiped clean.

Another excellent investment would be a ceramic infra-red lamp. When a guinea pig is a bit under the weather then the best treatment you can give is to apply controlled heat. Lamps can be attached to a hospital cage kept for this purpose; a thermostat into the lamp's wiring circuit, together with a reliable thermometer, completes your hospital unit.

The stockroom should contain a good working surface to prepare food and place stock on for routine health checks. Plenty of storage cupboards and bins to keep oats and food dry and safe from vermin will also be needed. Be sure that your stockroom is always dry and free from drafts.

Equally important is the fact that a hot stuffy stockroom will increase the risk of disease spreading rapidly, should it occur. Windows and ventilation points—both high up and low down—are thus essential. These should be covered with a wire mesh so that they can be opened in the warmer months without the risk of mice, rats or other unwanted visitors entering. The mesh thus needs to be of small hole diameter which would ideally be 1.25 cm (½ in) square. Finally, it is useful to number all of your hutches so that these can appear on record cards of your stock—a good breeder will keep very detailed records of all that happens in the stockroom as this will be important to future breeding operations.

Guinea pigs make delightful pets, being easy to care for and relatively undemanding.

Stock Selection

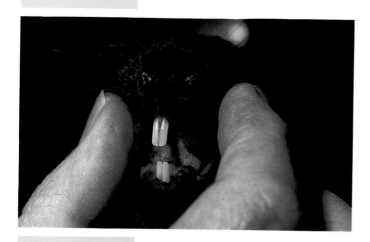

One of the many things you should check when purchasing a guinea pig is the animal's teeth. They should be sound and unbroken.

When purchasing one's initial stock there are numerous considerations to be made before preparing the accommodations already discussed. Is the guinea pig to be kept as a single pet, or along with two or three others? Is there any interest in breeding? If so, will this just be of an informal nature (to supply friends or the local pet shop with surplus animals) or do you want to breed specific varieties with the hopes of exhibiting the best of these? Regardless of your objective, the robustness and health of your guinea pigs are of foremost importance and it is here that we focus our attention.

HEALTH

The first thing that you should observe is that the guinea pigs under consideration are moving about freely with no impediment whatsoever. Baby guineas will move at very high speed so any that cannot should be ruled out. Next, pick up the guinea pig and inspect it carefully, going over the body a section at a time.

Head—The eyes should be round, bright, and clear, showing no signs of discharge. The nose will be relatively dry, maybe just a little moist but certainly with no indication that it is discharging liquid or has any sign of scabs. The ears will be soft and clean. The teeth will be in line: the top touching but just overlapping the bottom incisors. This is most important.

Body—This should be cylindrical, firm yet supple.

A baby guinea should not be fat or skinny. The coat should be fine and silky smooth with no bald patches nor any evidence of unwanted parasites (such as lice, mites or fleas). Incidentally, rodents bred in captivity are remarkably free of fleas so any with them really have been subjected to very unhygienic accommodation. Brush the fur against its lie to check for parasites and be sure that the coat springs back to its normal position. Check the underbelly of the animal for signs of sores or other abrasions to the skin. In the case of the Abyssinian guinea, the coat will feel harsh, which is how it should be.

Feet—These should be well-formed with all toes present.

Rump—This should be nicely rounded with no bones protruding from the frame of the body. The vent area should be clean and showing no signs of fecal staining or clogged matter, which would also indicate a problem.

Once you are satisfied that your selection is healthy, then have another good look at the guinea as it runs around just to satisfy yourself on this account.

WHERE TO PURCHASE

Your local pet shop will have suitable specimens on display. Some will be crossbreeds but they should also have purebreeds available, though they might not be of the caliber needed for breeding or exhibiting. As a beginner you will not have to be concerned about the "show quality" of your guinea pig.

The guinea pig that you select should be alert and interested in his surroundings.

19

Cleanliness—When purchasing from pet shops only give your custom to those which clearly keep their livestock in spacious and clean cages. In recent years, pet shops have become even better than they used to be. The modern pet shop will be free of overbearing animal odor and everything will be neatly racked just like a supermarket—these are the ones to patronize as they are obviously prepared to invest in offering you a first class service, and are concerned with customer satisfaction. Their stock may be just that little bit more expensive and it is surely worth the added cost to know you have purchased from a reliable source.

BREEDING STOCK

If you require high quality stock with good breeding and exhibiting potential, then you must buy direct from a breeder. Your pet shop may know one but if not, you can visit a county fair or a guinea show to see the many varieties and possibly purchase one from an exhibitor. If you intend on breeding, it is certainly advantageous to shop around in order to get a good idea of how each variety ideally looks.

THINK AHEAD

If you like all types of guinea pig, then here are a few extra thoughts:

1. If a given variety is very popular in your area, this can be useful as you can keep in touch with the breeder in case you require additional stock as you develop your own strain. However, one drawback is that competition at shows will be very strong with so many experienced people participating and surplus stock will have to be competitively priced as it will not be in short supply.

2. If you select a less popular variety, then maybe you can build a bit of a name locally in this variety and may be more successful at exhibitions. Further, surplus stock may command a higher price than the average popular variety, and there may be a waiting list of interested buyers. On the other hand, the variety may be more difficult to breed or

maybe they'll not sell so well.

It will certainly pay you to ponder these aspects. If you do plan to breed, then you should purchase a good trio (one boar and two sows) from a known, reliable, and successful breeder— remember it costs no more to feed and keep quality stock than it does to keep an inferior one, so the extra initial outlay will be repaid ten-fold, and even quality strains tend to not be very expensive. Do not go out, however, waving your checkbook in an attempt to buy the very best of stock, as this is not sound policy. If you do, then you will certainly be unable to breed to that same level and may be disappointed when your stock fails to win at the same level of competition (you will also quickly gain the dubious reputation of being a checkbook breeder and this can be difficult to shrug off). No, what you want is very sound stock from which you can breed winners as you gain experience so that the success, as it comes, is 100% yours, a much better feeling altogether. Good breeders are usually very honest and if

you tell them what your plans are, they will supply you with stock of appropriate quality. Don't go bargain hunting because, if you do, you will end up with stock that reflects the price you pay.

In concluding this chapter, I will again stress the need not to rush into a purchase— especially if breeding is planned. Take your time, do your research of breeders carefully, and do not start off with too many guinea pigs, no matter how strong the temptation. Once underway, you will want to add stock but, by then, you will have a much better idea of what you want to build on.

A black Dutch cavy. The Dutch cavy has a set pattern with a white background, similar to the Dutch rabbit.

Feeding

Rabbits, with which guinea pigs are often kept, can produce this vitamin and, as a result, rabbit foods that are commercially prepared are not fortified with vitamin C. If only such foods are fed to the guineas, sickness will result. Guinea pigs derive their vitamin C from greenfoods, which must be supplied.

Guinea pigs, along with most other rodents, are very easy animals to feed, providing one uses a degree of common sense about the matter. Their food should always be fresh, clean and represent each of the basic constituents required for healthy growth and resistance to disease. With this latter point in mind, it should be mentioned that guinea pigs are somewhat unusual because, unlike most other mammals, they appear not to be able to manufacture vitamin C in their bodies. This important vitamin prevents numerous ailments and must be available.

VARIETY

The good keepers will always ensure their animals receive a balanced variety of foods as this prevents the stock's becoming over fussy in its eating habits, and ensures that all basic ingredients are contained in the diet—it further reduces the risk of an ailment being caused by an excess of one type of food. For example, some plants have a laxative effect while others have a purgative one (as does roughage). Therefore, variety balances the two out and ensures a good constitution. We will go through all of the food types and discuss their benefits to your guinea pigs and, provided you supply examples from each of the groups, you should have no need to worry over your pet's dietary needs as these will be complete.

CEREALS

The popular cereals, such as crushed oats, bran, barley, wheat, and maize, are high in carbohydrate content and these compounds are made up of sugars, starch and cellulose. On oxidization within the body, the compounds release energy for normal muscular activity, generating heat in the process. Excess carbohydrates are converted into fats which are laid down in tissue to provide both insulation and a reserve source of energy. Cereals are normally supplied to guinea pigs in a mixed form which may also contain a number of the larger seeds of plants, such as sunflower. Ready-mixed bags can be purchased from your local pet store, but these can often prove wasteful as your pets will pick out the preferred items.

With only one or two guinea pigs, this will not really amount to much

money, but if a number are kept, it will clearly pay you to check out which foods your guinea pigs prefer, and purchase these individually to make your own mix.

Of course, any product that is made from cereals can also be fed to your pets, so that toasted wholemeal bread, cookies or biscuits, and breakfast cereals will all be eaten. When a dry mix is moistened with hot water, gravy stock, or milk, it is known as a mash. These make a pleasant change from an all dry diet and are especially appreciated by sows with young to rear.

When preparing a mash, you can mix into it various small seeds such as millet and canary seed that are rich in carbohydrates. Sunflower seeds are high in fat and protein content as are

Young guinea pigs. Guinea pigs are curious little animals that will delight you with their antics.

peanuts (unsalted only) and pine nuts. Guinea pigs will vary in their attitude to these latter seeds but, by all means, try them together with any other shelled nuts such as almonds, Brazils, and walnuts—these are expensive but if it is only for one or two pets then they will add variety to the daily menu and might become a much cherished treat.

PROTEIN

It can be seen from the table of foodstuff contents that the protein needs of guinea pigs will also come from cereals, with a small percentage coming from greenfoods and root vegetables. Proteins are needed to build bodily tissue as well as to replace that which has worn out. It can be seen from the table that fats also associate with protein: fatty oils are needed both to give insulation and to assist in the absorption of

vitamins into the body. Certain foods are lacking in amino acids, the building blocks of proteins and, while the importance of these missing amino acids may not be as essential to guinea pigs and other chiefly herbivorous mammals, nonetheless, they can be supplied through cheese, milk, fish and similar animal product proteins. These can be mixed with a mash. There is little doubt that, in the wild state, guinea pigs would eat a small amount of animal protein in the form of invertebrates such as worms, together with any that are clinging to vegetation eaten. The total consumed would be small but sufficient to meet the metabolic needs of the animal.

VITAMINS

Vitamins are a number of compounds that assist, in all sorts of different ways, the body to operate as it should. A deficiency of any will create problems as will an excess, equally so. These excess vitamins will be passed out of the body in urine or feces while others will be absorbed into the tissues where they will upset

other vital systems; they may well have a counter-effect on other vitamins so the liberal use of vitamin supplements should be avoided and supplied only on veterinary advice.

GREENFOOD

Fruit and vegetables are nature's richest source of vitamins, and provided a balanced supply is given, the total vitamin needs of your

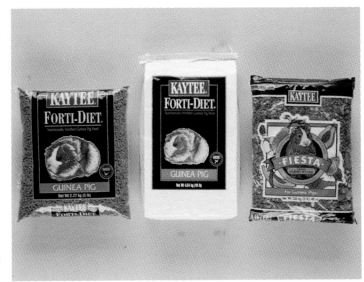

Constituents of Various Foodstuffs by Percentages					
Food	Carbohydrate	Fat	Mineral	Protein	
Wheat	74	2	2	11	Note: The percentages
White Millet	66	4	3	12	quoted are
Maize	63	7	2	10	typical but may vary in
Oats	56	5	2	11	individual
Barley	70	2	2	10	samplings
Sunflower Seeds	21	45	3	20	dependent on
Peanuts	19	45	5	25	age when
Pine Nuts	12	45	4	30	stored, variety, and
Vetch	50	2	3	23	the area in
Apple	15	0	1.5	.5	which grown.
Lettuce	2	.2	1.8	1	Water
Dandelion	10.6	1	1	2.4	contents not shown.
Carrot	9.6	.01	2.5	1.2	

guinea pigs should be adequately met. Because vitamins are relatively unstable compounds they do not store too well, and this is especially true of vitamin C—the one highly important need of guinea pigs. With this in mind, any greenfood given should always be as fresh as possible, as it quickly sours. And although the animals are unlikely to eat it once it sours, soured vegetation can attract parasites and harmful bacteria and thus should be removed once pets have had their fill. Smaller portions frequently are better than a large mound of greenfood which the animals may stuff themselves on and develop digestive upsets.

There is a vast range of vegetables to offer your guineas; some of these include Brussels sprouts, cabbage, peas, broccoli, spinach, celery, cauliflower, and kale. Always select the fresh green outer leaves which contain the most nourishment and are preferred by guinea pigs. The stalks complete with roots will also be welcome. All vegetables should be carefully washed to remove any potentially dangerous chemical sprays. This is extremely important in the case of wild plants that may have been collected on road

Treat foods such as those shown here will be greatly relished by a guinea pig and will add a good bit of variety to the diet. Photo courtesy Vitakraft.

verges, as apart from crop spraying chemicals they are likely to have been contaminated by motor fumes or fouled by dogs.

Root vegetables enjoyed by guineas will include carrots, beetroot, swede, parsnip, turnips, and similar items that you yourself would eat. Avoid bulbs such as tulips, daffodils, or any plant that grows from a bulb. The best guide is that if you can eat it, so can your pets, so onions, garlic, leeks, and the like are all possibilities. Of course some pets will refuse some of these while others will accept them in small amounts, especially if chopped into small pieces and given in a mixed salad with other fruits and vegetables you know they enjoy.

The most readily available wild plant, if one could call it that, will be fresh grass cuttings from your lawn. (Be sure that it is fresh and has not been chemically treated.) Do not overdo it as too much will quickly give your pet an upset stomach. Of the wild plants found in gardens and countryside, the list is enormous but may include: blackberry, dandelion, chickweed, comfrey,

plantain, nettle, shepherd's purse, yarrow, clover, sowthistle, groundsel, dock, mallow, hawkweed, cow parsley, ground elder, and others. The ones to avoid are buttercup (but this is rendered harmless if in a dried state among hay), ragwort, hemlock, lily of the valley, deadly nightshade, charlock (often grows with cereal crops) bracken, and bryony. You are advised to invest in a good book on wild plants of your area—and one which is illustrated in color—so that you can be familiar with the various plants. Some breeders cultivate wild plants in a small area of their yards and gardens and this is a good idea. Again, feed the entire plant including roots— washing and shaking them before feeding.

Potatoes are not normally appreciated by guinea pigs but they can be boiled and then mixed in with a mash in small amounts. Likewise, meats are not given to guinea pigs though I have noted that when we mix up table scraps any meat included will be eaten if it is only in small quantities. (We once had a rabbit that was very fond of

"Root vegetables enjoyed by guineas will include carrots, beetroot, swede, parsnip, turnips, and similar items that you yourself would eat."

pork pies and the guineas which shared his home would nibble bits of this as well, and they were certainly very fit little animals.) Do not feed sweet items such as candies to your pets for, while they may well acquire a taste for them, they are totally unneeded.

HAY

I have singled out hay for special consideration as it is so important to guinea pigs both as a rich source of roughage and as a bedding material—being far superior to straw on both accounts. Try and obtain a good clean source of supply in bulk, by the bale if you have numerous guineas; if only a single pet is kept then your pet shop will supply various sized packages. A good idea is to use quality straw as a bed base and then add hay to this each day. By the following morning, most of the hay will have been consumed. If your pets are housed outdoors, then the amount of hay should be increased over the winter months, for it is essential that guinea pigs be housed snugly.

WATER

Your guinea pigs should always have available to them a good fresh supply of water, regardless of how much greenfood they have. Contrary to old wives' tales, these animals drink quite a lot, especially when the weather gets warmer. It should be changed daily and is a means of supplying tonics and medicines, though not a very reliable way because you cannot gauge how much has been drunk.

PELLETS

Commercially prepared pellets are available from pet stores and these contain all the required ingredients for a nutritionally balanced diet. If guinea pigs are fed purely on pellets, you will notice an increase in the amount of water they drink.

Pellets prepared specifically for rabbits are not fortified with vitamin C, which is essential to guinea pigs. This can be provided by additional greenfoods or can be given via the drinking water which has been supplemented by special vitamin rich powders. It is possible today to purchase pellets for rabbits which have also been treated with various antibacterial substances but these may not always be beneficial to guinea pigs; should you keep two such pets together, check with your supplier about this matter. There are numerous brands of pellets available and cavies differ in their tastes, so one brand may be preferred to another (a point to consider when changing brands).

Pellets can be soaked in warm water and mixed with a mash to give it extra nutritional value when sows have piglets to feed. I would never feed an all-pellet diet to my guinea pigs because I believe that eating various foods has a social and therapeutic value to animals,

A trio of young guinea pigs that are littermates. Notice the variation in their color and markings.

which is absent with pellets. They are useful additives provided they are not fed in excess alongside a normal diet because, while they look small, they are highly concentrated.

WHEN TO FEED

The feeding routine will be governed by the hours when it is most convenient for you. Ideally, three feeds per day should be given. The early morning feed will be of mixed dried oats, plus baked bread or the like, together with greenfood and some fruit. About midday, a few root vegetables and any table scraps can be given, and then in the early evening a mash plus some wild plants can be fed. I prefer to feed the mash at night because the temperature is lower and such food quickly goes off if given during the daytime.

The amounts to feed should be such that there are just a few pieces left over to be removed. If nothing is left, you are underfeeding, and if lots are left, you are giving too much or giving foods they clearly do not like. My guineas always have oats and water available to them 24 hours per day.

It is interesting to compare the differing reactions of guineas and rabbits at feeding time. The guineas will waddle towards their compound fence at high speed and squeal as loud as they can while running in little circles in front of me; the rabbits will sprint up to the fence and stretch up on their rear legs, twitch their heads and ears before sprinting off at high speed round their pen in obvious excitement of the meal to come. Once a meal is given, both will inspect it first; the rabbits will eat where they stand but the guinea pigs will snatch a choice morsel and dash off a few feet to eat by themselves. Only when feeding on grass do they stay put and work their way through the little quantity supplied. These little characteristics and many others go unnoticed if your guinea pigs are exclusively confined to cage life.

Remember, feed a wide variety of foods, feed at regular times, and always take note of the particular favorite items of each individual. This way, when one appears a little sickly, you will know what to tempt it with, and if it refuses its favorite food, then you will know something is really amiss.

31

Guinea Pig Varieties

With so many varieties to choose from, it is worthwhile making every effort to see as many of these as possible before deciding which is the one for you. Although many are illustrated in this book, a visit to one or two exhibitions is strongly recommended. Guinea pigs are divided into two major groups based on their color and coat types, and these are as follows:

1. *Self varieties*—These all have short smooth coats and the coat color is the same throughout the guinea pig.

2. *Non-self varieties*—Here the coat length may be long or short, bristly or velvetlike; the color is either uniform or of two or more shades which may be arranged in any number of patterns on the animal.

The guinea pig is judged according to a standard of points which dictates the importance of certain features, and the overall way a cavy is put together in respect of its conformation is known as its type. Generally, the self varieties are of a better type than are the non-self, with the self black possibly being the best of all guinea pigs if considered in terms of its color and type.

BODY AND SIZE

The shape of the guinea pig is much as described for the wild cavy but the head is considerably larger, the foreface should be blunt, and the head, broad. There is no obvious neck and the shoulders are large leading into a sleek body with a well-rounded rump. There is no visible tail, though the guinea pig does have one much reduced and subcutaneous. Body length can vary considerably being from 22-34 cm (8½-13½ in).

THE SELF VARIETIES

Black

A good exhibition self black is a most impressive guinea pig. The color is jet black all over and any indication of another color—such as white or red in the coat—would give such an example little chance in a show due to strong competition in this color. The pendant, petal-like ears should show no signs of damage. As with most guinea pigs, it can be difficult to really judge a good example until it is fully mature. The coat should be sleek and glossy. It is possible to combine the crest mutation with the self guinea pigs and these are always popular. As a general rule, it will be found that sows tend to be of better type than boars, and usually carry a more refined coat, any tendency towards coarseness being a bad fault in all self varieties.

White

There are two forms of the white: the first being the true albino, which is devoid of dark pigments and thus has red eyes; and the second is a dark-eyed white in which some dark pigment can be seen in the ears and possibly elsewhere. The albino form is obviously a purer white as dark-eyed whites have the problem that, as one tries to intensify the white, the eye color also becomes lighter—whereas the object is to achieve a truly black eye color. Whites tend to exhibit a yellowish hue to them; this is due to traces of pigment still being evident in the hair. A further problem with dark-eyed whites is that selective breeding for color intensity will often result in a loss of type—this is a problem with any self exhibiting a very pale color.

"The shape of the guinea pig is much as described for the wild cavy but the head is considerably larger, the foreface should be blunt, and the head, broad."

Chocolate

The chocolate should be dark, not light as in milk chocolate, the eyes are ruby. This color has been around a long while but does not enjoy its former popularity—no doubt due to the emergence of the many other color shades. It would be a pity to see the chocolate disappear, and although it is still kept in reasonable numbers at this time, it can be surprising just how quickly varieties vanish once their popularity starts to decrease beyond a given point. The quality of coat in this color is usually excellent so it can be used to good effect in other colors.

Red

This is another example of a color which does not enjoy its former popularity. Ideally, it should be a mahogany red and the eyes, ruby. Often one sees white and black hairs in the coat which also shows variation in the depth of red. The difficulty of succeeding with this color is further intensified by the coat's changing at different stages in the animal's life.

Golden

There are dark and ruby-eyed variants of this color, the latter being the more commonly seen. The shade of color required should be on the red side of golden rather than the light and, indeed, deep goldens could easily be mistaken for reds. The undercoat should match the top color for best effect. In the US, this color is known as orange.

Beige

The beige is not the easiest color to produce and defining the color as "like real beige cloth" assumes agreement on what is real beige cloth! I will leave it to the reader to decide what the color should be, but I would describe beige guinea pigs as ranging from a dark cream through to a diluted orange, and within a single litter, one may see just such variety. Beige guineas are normally darker when young, and they vary in the amount of white hairs that are evident, so it is a difficult color to succeed in, the more so because type is not always good. The usual pairing is light to dark in the hopes of getting the right shade about midway between the two. The colors do not mix like paint, however, as one may think might happen. The reason mid-points are achieved involves the genes that control the color showing continuous variation from light to dark; thus the hope is that one is able to obtain an equal distribution of the two. In theory it should be possible to obtain a more uniform color with selective breeding within a strain, but paler creams are considered more desirable. In the US, the dark creams are called buff. Traces of yellow are undesirable but almost impossible to avoid given the make-up of the cream; for this reason, only the very best examples will make the grade in top class competition. Pairing light to dark is not normally

An assortment of various color varieties. Guinea pigs are lovable little characters, each with a personality all its own.

this presupposes that officials are able to be more specific about what shade really is the most desirable, which is difficult to state.

Cream

The cream color is popular and seen in a variety of shades from very pale to quite dark; the eyes are ruby. The undercoat should match the topcoat and the recommended yet a good dark cream will be of value in a stud in order to maintain vigor and to retain the right depth of cream. Continual pairings of the lightest creams will not, in fact, produce the best types as time goes on.

Lilac

The lilac is nothing like the color you might be

imagining and is a sort of grayish beige. It is still very much in its infancy as a color. The dilution of the black gene produces blue and, in theory, mating self blue with chocolate will produce blacks in the first generation. If these are then paired it should be possible to produce a reasonable lilac—but the chances are only 1 in 16. Such lilacs should then be paired with the blues and chocolates, when the number of lilacs will dramatically increase. A better description of the color would be dove gray as most so-called lilacs would be disappointing to the average newcomer unaware of what the color was really like.

Blue

This color is not standardized in the UK and is a dilution of the black gene. It should be a dark blue with eyes of similar color, but these will normally appear black in most light. Blues are not seen at their best until they have fully matured. There is likely to be a ticking effect in this color and, while the dark blue is preferred, it may be that if the variety is to become well-established then a somewhat lighter shade will be needed. Otherwise blue will likely live in the shadow of the black which is a more strongly preferred color.

New Colors

There is no doubt that we will see a number of new colors in the selfs because as the dilution factor becomes better established and understood, so will the number of color re-combinations. Presently, the saffron, a pale yellow, is being developed. It is possible to combine the various modifications to the hair, such as the crest, the ridgeback, and the rex and satin coats, to any of the self colors, so that the potential permutations are considerable. However, it is in the next group of varieties that we will most certainly

A golden American crested sow. Note the lustrous quality of the coat.

see the greatest number of new ones created.

NON-SELF VARIETIES

This large group contains all varieties that are not self colored and which have modifications to their coat type, thus a bicolored guinea pig, or one exhibiting a pattern of two or more colors, is a non-self.

Abyssinian

The Abyssinian guinea pig has long been popular as a show guinea and as a pet. However, really good show specimens are not easy to breed because the standard is very demanding in respect to how the rosettes, for which the breed is famous, are placed on the body. The hair should be as coarse as possible—the only guinea pig to have this requirement at this time—and this enables the stiff hairs to project out from the body to create the rosettes which should ideally radiate from a pinpoint center.

There should be four rosettes on the body, two hip rosettes and two on the rump and shoulders. The ridge which starts on the crown of the head should go down the guinea pig's back

and, for this to be so, it means the rosettes must be placed so that the crests of those on the body meet to create the ridge. The length of the hair should be up to 3.8 cm (1½ in).

In many pet Abyssinians, it will be found that the rosettes are often rather flat, some are missing or poorly placed, thus giving an unbalanced look to the guinea. However, these will still make fine pets. It is important in this variety to handle them on a regular basis because some strains have gained a bit of a bad reputation for biting and being rather aggressive with other guinea pigs—this is noticed more in the boars. This should not deter would-be pet owners because, in most cases, they are as reliable as other varieties; it is possible they have a greater predisposition to aggression but whether or not this actually develops will be determined by how they are brought up.

Color is not the major consideration in this variety but if you plan to exhibit, I would stick with the darker varieties such as brindle or tortoiseshell and white. Be cognizant that the lighter the overall coloring is, the more difficult it is to retain stiffness in the rosettes. The dark selfs, while superior in coat to light selfs, are inferior in coat to the brindles.

Peruvian

The Peruvian guinea pig, the complete opposite to the Abyssinian, has a coat that is extremely long and silky. It may be up to 51 cm (20 in) in length and this will entail very considerable work on your behalf if you should consider this variety (which I suggest you do not). Breeders of guinea pigs have strong views on this variety and I am among those who feel it should never have been bred—or that a limit should have been placed on the length of hair it should have, thus allowing it to live a reasonably normal life.

A top show specimen is akin to a silky mop or wig

that is alive! It does seem to me that when we deprive an animal of its ability to see as it should, move freely as it should, breed as it should, and keep itself clean as it is naturally born to do, then we are pandering to our own egos without any thoughts whatsoever of the animal subjected to such misfortunes. This is not a situation unique to guinea pigs because no doubt the reader can name a number of comparable cases in other animals such as dogs, cats, goldfish, and birds where a feature has become exaggerated out of all reasonable proportions. In the case of the Peruvian, the examples of years ago had far shorter coats, but it seems that breeders are encouraged to produce ever longer coats in order to attain top winning status.

If a Peruvian is purchased as a pet, then the best course of action is that once the coat begins to become unmanageable, it should be trimmed right back so that your pet can see properly and can move without hindrance. This will make a dramatic difference to its future life. The show

Peruvian must be kept on paper rather than on sawdust or hay, otherwise its coat will become very tangled. Likewise, it will need grooming every day and special care so that it does not become soiled with feces. Many show examples will need to have their coats placed in special curlers in order to improve the waves which are desired, so that, one way or the other, it really is a variety for those who clearly do find it worthwhile breeding. Obviously, when sows are pregnant the coat must be trimmed back considerably; otherwise the babies will find it somewhat difficult to feed from their mother. The coat of the Peruvian is in fact the development of the rosettes of the Abyssinian, of which it is a long-coated variant.

Sheltie

Somewhat similar to the Peruvian is the Sheltie, but here we see a long-coated, self equivalent (because it is available in many colors, it is not a self as such). The coat of the Sheltie is not quite as

The guinea pig is cobby in type, which means that its rump or hindquarters is rounded.

long as that of the Peruvian and does not grow over the face, so the guinea pig is able to see as normal. However, coat length has been increasing with passing years so it now has much the same problems as the Peruvian in its management and cannot realistically be recommended to the average beginner.

It is essential that the Sheltie's coat is groomed regularly or trimmed back regularly because both the Sheltie and the Peruvian really do look like very sorry animals when this is not done, and, as a result will lead quite miserable lives.

Agouti

The agouti-marked guinea pig is of course a long established variety, and while the silver and the golden shades are the most popular, other colors are rapidly gaining support: the orange, the cinnamon, the salmon, and the lemon, together with the argente are such examples.

The agouti markings are the result of colored bands on the hair. The silver has a black-blue base hair which is tipped with silver giving the characteristic ticking—in the case of the golden it is a brownish base with tips of gold. In the case of the cinnamon, there is a double banding created by the fact that the silver tips to the otherwise golden hair are capped with brown to give a pleasing effect. The Silver Agouti may well lose some of its former popularity with the emergence of new varieties, but it is to be hoped not so much that it becomes a rarity. As with other agoutis, always look for evenness of ticking, and in the case of the silver, the standards reached in past years have been extremely high. This can have a negative effect on a variety's popularity in that newcomers find success difficult so are tempted into the newer colors where maybe competition is not quite so fierce.

Roan

The roan variety should not be confused by the beginner for an agouti—they are quite different. In the roan we have two colors which are independent of each other in the hairs, which intermingle to give a beautiful mottled effect as seen in the roan Cocker Spaniels. The blue roan has a

blue-black head and ears and the body is ideally of an even mixture of blue and white, with blue feet. The evenness of the roan markings can be very variable in individuals. When breeding this variety it is usual to pair a roan with its base color, so a blue would be mated to a self blue, a black to a self black and so on. The reason for this is that if roans are paired together a percent of the young will be whites which will be affected by blindness—this is also seen when merled colors are paired together in dogs, and in both cases is caused by a lethal factor in the genetic make-up. Such animals are usually also deaf and probably sterile. The genetic reason is that as long as the lethal gene is in single quantity, no problems will be evident; it is when they double up that effects will show.

There is a roan variety known as the strawberry, which is actually a red-orange color intermingled with white hairs. When the roan becomes more patchy it is termed dapple roan. Good roans are not easily come by but are extremely impressive guinea pigs.

A self lilac sow and her young.

Dalmatian

The dalmatian is named for the dog of this pattern which exhibits black, blue, or dark gray spotting on its coat. The head is black with a white blaze and the feet are the color of the spotting. This variety is still being developed and does not compare with the dog in terms of its spotting, which is more akin to blotches, but in the coming years it will be refined by breeding to the most desirable examples. The method of breeding is the same as for roans. You will find considerable variation in the quality of dalmatians, both in markings and in type; however, this is to be expected when a new variety is being established, as one must breed with well-marked animals which may not have the most desirable type. Once a variety has become well-established for its color, or pattern, or coat variation, breeders are able to concentrate on the overall conformation, but this takes many years so if you prefer guinea pigs of good type then it is advisable that you select the long established varieties.

Himalayan

In whatever animal it appears, the Himalayan mutation is always popular. It is seen in cats, rabbits, and mice and is characterized by the animal's having dark extremities—nose, ears and feet (and tail, where applicable)—which contrast the white body. However, getting pure white bodies can be difficult and often there is a creamish hue to the coat, more noticeable on the back and sides.

The Himalayan mutation is, in effect, an albino which retains pigmentation and is a temperature–sensitive mutation. By this is meant that pigment is partially retained on the coldest parts of the body, those furthest from the heart. The result of this is that if exposed to sunlight the color will fade because the extremities will obviously become warmer. Likewise, the ears are usually darker than the facemask, which may in turn be darker than the feet.

When they are first born and for some weeks afterwards, Himalayan guinea pigs appear all white as the color begins to develop, feet first, as the weeks go by. When breeding Himalayans, care must be exercised that when selecting for white body, the dark points are not reduced; the same being true in reverse, in that improved color means a loss of whiteness. A good cross would be Himalayan × true self white (i.e., albino) as this should retain good white. The only color available at this time is the chocolate which can be either dark (when it is called black) or light (when it is called chocolate). When distinguishing between the two is not this obvious, the color of the ears will give you the best guide as to which it should be classed. It will not be too long before blue points appear. As a point of interest, there may well be two separate mutations being regarded as one, in that, within rabbits, we see a very clear line of demarcation between the points and the body color, whereas in Siamese cats, it is more a case of merging one into the other, and in the latter, the body color is off-white. However, it could equally be a case that the single mutation for Himalayan displays variation depending on other factors in the animal's genetic color make-up.

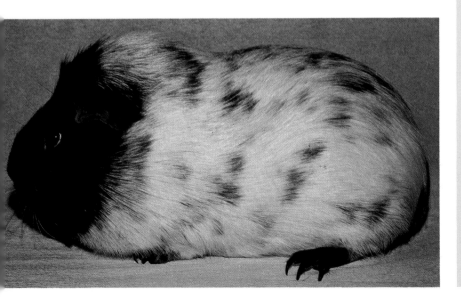

A Dalmatian sow. This variety is a mutation of the self black.

Dutch

The dutch pattern markings of the rabbit are probably well-known to most readers and comprise a colored band on the back end of the animal with a similar colored head which carries a white blaze coming to a point as it passes between the ears, before opening up to cover the front end of the animal. The rear toes should be white.

Obtaining straight lines of demarcation between the color and the white is not easy, and much stock will fail in this respect. Likewise, obtaining a good blaze of the desired shape is also difficult and in a single litter all will be different to some degree. The area of color should ideally be greater than that of the white. Color may be black, chocolate, golden, agouti, or any recognized one but the black and the golden are possibly the more popular.

Tortoiseshell and White

The tortie and white is always a popular pet guinea pig but breeding a good show specimen that meets the standard is all but impossible—as a result any that approach the ideal are suitable for exhibition. This is a tricolored guinea combining black, red, and white. These colors should form squares of color which alternate down one side of the body then come up the other side in another sequence, meeting in a straight line down the center of the back.

You can imagine how difficult this is to achieve, and it is usually luck if a well-marked example turns up in a litter. However, this very fact adds a bit of excitement to their breeding, and in any case they are always very impressive looking guinea pigs with lots of appeal.

Tortoiseshell

This old variety has the same demands as the last one, but there is no white involved. This should make things easier, you might think, but it does not. In fact, it could be said to be even more difficult because often there are undesirable white hairs in the fur. It is not a popular guinea pig and is comparatively rare, possibly lacking some of the appeal of the tortie and white which looks much more colorful.

Bicolor

In this variety we have the same pattern as in the tortoiseshell but the colors are any combination other than red and black. There is black and white, cream and black, red and white, chocolate and white, and so on. A tricolored variety is now being bred that would combine white with any other two colors but red and black (both of which can be featured but not together as this would be a tortie and white).

Brindle

The brindle is not a popular variety but combines red and black in smoothcoated guineas. Ideally, these colors should blend in the most even manner possible throughout the coat. Generally, it will be found that red and black as a single combination is never that popular because the guinea pigs which also have white or another light color in the fur are always in greater demand.

Magpie

The magpie is one of the new varieties and is becoming quite popular. In this guinea pig, the coat is black and white arranged in bands on the body; the lines of demarcation between black and white are not yet clean as in other animal magpies but are a mixture of both hair colors to which blue is added to create a roan zone.

Harlequin

Another new variety is the harlequin in which three colors are arranged in bands around the body. This is a difficult variety to breed to a high standard but does offer a challenge to those wishing to be involved in the early development of a variety.

Rex Coats

The rex mutation, named for that seen in rabbits, affects the guard hairs which do not grow. The effect is to create a soft woolly hair. In the rabbit, this mutation has been carefully bred for many years so that the fur has a smooth velvet feel to it, but in the guinea pig, the effect is presently such that the coat is initially wavy, then softer with age. With selective breeding, there is

"Another new variety is the harlequin, in which three colors are arranged in bands around the body."

no doubt that a velvetlike smoothness will eventually be achieved. This mutation, like others that affect the coat, is not in any way linked to the color of the guinea pig, so that the rex coat can be attained in any color or pattern.

Satin

If you think that the average good smooth-coated guinea pig has a glossy coat then wait until you see a good satin. Here the coat really excels in its silky texture and sheen. Once again, the satin mutation can be transferred to any of the colors and coat patterns.

Crest

The crest mutation has now been available for a number of years and should ideally be a complete rosette on the crown of the head, radiating from a pinpoint center. In the US, where the mutation first appeared, the crest must be of a differing color to the body, but in the UK this is optional. Most color varieties are now available with crests, the quality of which can vary from excellent to rather poor.

Ridgeback

The ridgeback is a recent development and here, as the name implies, the hair of the back forms a ridge, which ideally should be complete. It is still very much in its infancy.

Mutations

The reader may wonder just how mutations come about so a few words on them seem appropriate. Animals are continually mutating which is nature's way of testing out modifications to see if these are to the benefit of a species. In most cases, they are not so they rarely become established in wild stock. Those which are only very minor will be retained and they account for speciation— the formation of new species—but these take thousands of years to develop. More radical mutations are those which suddenly appear and change a visual feature, such as hair type, size, or color. What happens is that the genes which control the feature are affected by radiation, cosmic rays, or other factors not yet fully understood. The result of this is that the genes quite suddenly express themselves in a differing manner to that which they previously did.

Once a gene has mutated, it will then act as a normal gene and continue to express itself in a predictable manner—but of course for the new feature.

The incidence of mutations always increases in domestically bred stock in ratio with the number of animals bred in the overall population—as a general rule. A mutation can happen at any time—you cannot plan it—and it can happen in any animal, so that it is quite a random situation that could turn up in *your* stock. It has often happened that a mutation is not always recognized by breeders who, seeing an animal exhibiting an unusual feature or color, think of it merely as a runt or freak and thus ignore it. In other cases, usually when it is pleasing, it will be selectively bred for.

The news is not always good, however, because some mutations also affect the internal metabolism of the animal in a negative manner, and this is not always immediately apparent. In other cases, the mutation may be linked to a lethal factor in which the young die either in their

mother's womb or early in their lives. Alternately, they may have a disability or be sterile, depending on the potency of the so-called lethal factor. The whole area of mutations is quite fascinating and those readers who wish to understand this in greater depth are recommended to purchase any sound book on basic genetics; it is not important that it relates to the guinea pig, as the basis of heredity and mutations applies to all life forms. Once the fundamentals are grasped, it is merely a case of inserting the known genetic information on the guinea pig to be able to calculate the results from crosspairing the numerous mutations seen in our pets.

An average guinea pig litter will consist of two or three young. Occasionally, larger litters do occur.

Breeding

The breeding of guinea pigs is a most fascinating aspect of the hobby, and seeing one's first litter of piglets scampering about their hutch is a most exciting time; the whole family will very much enjoy such a moment. Guinea pigs are reliable breeders rather than prolific, and you will thus not have large numbers to sell off as do owners of most rodents. As explained in an earlier chapter it is certainly recommended that you commence with a purebreed and with good quality stock, which will be a better long-term investment. Before contemplating breeding, do be sure you have adequate and suitable spare stock cages so you are not at a loss to know where to put youngsters as they develop.

BREEDING AGE

Guinea pigs are sexually mature by the time they are about seven weeks old, but you should not allow such immature animals to breed as the young may be weakly as a result and it could likely ruin the development and breeding potential of the parents. A sow can be bred from once she has passed the age of three months and no later than say ten months. Although she can have a first litter after ten months, it will carry greater health risks to her because her pelvic bones may well have become very rigid, which may result in difficulties in giving birth. The sow can breed until she is about four years old.

A good breeding age for a boar would be about five to six months as by this age he will have become quite mature and had time to develop his muscle and vigor; I feel it is never wise to use boars too early and have always had good strong youngsters as a result.

BREEDING CONDITION

It is important that both the boar and the sow are only allowed to mate if they are in superb breeding condition. They should be neither over nor underweight as this can only result in the piglets having less than ideal parents. This is especially so in the case of the sow. The proposed pairs should be given plenty of exercise in the weeks prior to the mating period, and an increase in the amount of protein the sow receives will be beneficial. The addition of some powdered calcium mix into the mash will ensure that the sow will not be deficient in this important metallic element which is needed by the youngsters in order to develop strong bones.

PAIRS OR COLONY BREEDING

There are numerous options open to you on how you wish to breed your guinea pigs. The boar may be run with a single sow or two, three, or four. Also, the boar can be safely left with the sows up to and even after the piglets are born. Most boars are extremely good fathers and very caring and tolerant towards babies; one occasionally finds a less than ideal father who may attack the youngsters and thus should be removed.

The problem with leaving the boar with the sow after the babies are born is that as soon as this happens the female may conceive again, and this is not desirable. It is therefore advised that he be removed just prior to immediately after the piglets appear. There are other potential problems when one keeps a number of females together and all having been

You can enjoy great pleasure from breeding your guinea pigs as pets or breeding pure breeds for exhibition.

mated. First, when a sow has her litter, the other sows will tend to mother it as well, and may become very excited about the event to the point that it could result in their aborting their own litter. Once each of the sows have had their litters the babies will quite happily feed from any sow, and it is possible that one sow may prove more popular than the others, thus she may be overtaxed by the demands made upon her. The colony system does have the singular advantage that, should a sow not have sufficient milk for her litter, this will not be felt by her babies, because feeding will be random within the sows of the group.

Should each of the sows be of the same variety and color there can be a problem of identification with the piglets unless they are marked with a temporary stain.

Possibly the most suitable method of breeding (assuming you wish a particular boar to cover a number of sows) is to run the boar with the sows for about 21 days and then separate the whole group into their own accommodations. If the sows are left too late before they go into separate housing they may become very concerned once split up from the boar and other sows, and in an advanced state of pregnancy, this is not desirable. At three weeks, you could always leave the boar in with one for a day or two while it settles into its new quarters, repeating the operation with the next sow.

BREEDING CYCLE AND GESTATION PERIOD

The female guinea pig will breed continuously throughout the year if so allowed. The estrus period is normally 16 days but can be a day or two longer, while the gestation period is 59-72 days. Exactly when a mating has taken place can be difficult to determine so the due date of the birth of piglets can only be approximate. You will notice the sow becoming fatter by about the fortieth day but not always, as some sows hardly reveal they are carrying babies until almost the last week before they give birth (especially if they are carrying only one or two babies).

"The female guinea pig will breed continuously throughout the year if so allowed."

50

THE BIRTH

More often than not the sow will give birth to her young during the night so the first you will know of things is when you see the babies the following morning.

An average litter will consist of two or three but larger litters may appear, though in such cases there may be one or two dead babies among these on many occasions. Guinea pigs are born fully furred and able to run around within hours of being born. Although they are capable of eating greenfood and oats almost from birth, it will be found that this is really only of a testing kind and it will be a few days before they tackle such foods seriously.

The sow has only two nipples but manages to suckle three or four babies without any problems as they automatically take turns at feeding. If a sow did have three or four babies, while another had only one, then it is beneficial to foster one from the larger to the smaller litter. Check that the foster mother accepts the new baby without any problems.

Both the sow and her

youngsters will appreciate bread soaked in milk during the first week or two, and the addition of malt extract, or similar highly nutritious foods mixed in with a mash will also give the piglets a good start in life. The young guinea pigs will be weaned from their mother by about the age of 18-32 days, this varying quite markedly within individuals, but 25 days would be a good average.

SEXING

The young guineas will be sexually mature by the age of about ten weeks so, after this

If you breed poor stock, it will take several generations simply to bring the quality of the guinea pigs up to acceptable breeding standards.

time, you should be thinking in terms of separating the sexes so to avoid premature matings. The sows can happily be kept together and will be no problem.

Young boars will coexist with each other for a short while longer but when the playful fighting starts to take on a more serious look then they must be separated for good. I have known of young boars living together in harmony for a considerable length of time, but there were no sows at all being kept by the owner, and the boars had a quite large compound and could avoid each other; this, however, is not a normal situation, as invariably boars fight very fiercely.

To sex guinea pigs you must carefully support them and turn them onto their backs in the palm of your hand. By very gently using your thumb and index finger, apply pressure to either side of the genital opening. If the guinea is a boar its penis will protrude; if not then it is a sow. Sexing is best done at about 6-8 weeks of age. In the case of older boars, you should be able to see the testicles.

HANDLING

Guinea pigs are much more nimble than rabbits so should be handled on a regular basis from an early age in order to overcome their inherent nervousness. The correct way to pick up a guinea is to slide your palm under its body so that your fingers pass between its legs, thus giving it no leverage to spring from. Your other hand then secures it in the region of the shoulders. The essential aspect is that its body must always be supported; never grasp it so that it is dangling, as this will merely prompt it to struggle and, being rump-heavy, it may slip from your grasp and badly injure itself as a result of a fall.

GUINEA PIGS WITH OTHER PETS

Guinea pigs are quite safe with rabbits, and a large guinea will also be reasonably safe with most cats, but considerable caution should be exercised whenever cats or dogs are around a guinea pig that is loose. Because guineas scamper off so quickly, they are likely to prompt the hunting instinct in these two carnivores who will immediately give chase to them and maybe bite them. Cats are especially dangerous because of their tendency to treat small guinea pigs as mice—thus clawing them. I would suggest, therefore, that when the guinea pig is loose your other pets are best kept away from them, and certainly children should be well-disciplined on this matter.

If guinea pigs are in a compound that is not covered with netting, they are at risk, the small ones in particular, of prowling, venatic feline creatures. This fact needs consideration. They are somewhat at less risk if such a pound includes a large active male rabbit and I have found most cats very cautious at entering pounds where such a male lives. The safest bet is to cover compounds with small-hole netting.

BREEDING THEORY

The object of a breeding program is to try and produce successive generations of guinea pigs that are superior to your initial stock for those features you wish to breed.

To achieve this, you must first of all keep very detailed records of all your matings. Such records should indicate which guinea pigs were paired, how many young were produced, how many were reared, and whether the sow was a good mother. It is

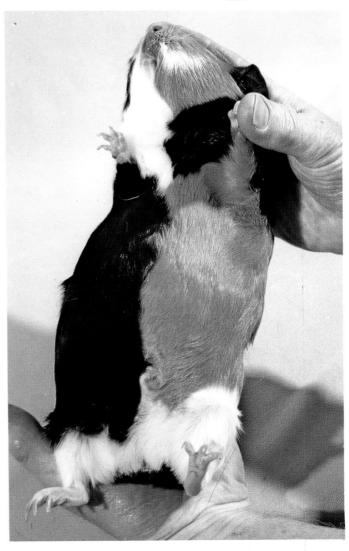

An underside view of a tortie and white cavy.

important not only that you breed from good looking animals, but also that you consider other inherited characteristics such as fertility, any tendency for sows to be aggressive towards offspring, any incidence of abnormal births or of deformed young, and similar examples. You want strong vigorous stock that will reliably reproduce its own kind. This should be your main objective at all times, so that improvements in type should never be at the expense of vigor, as this is a very short-term policy that will eventually create problems. Pursuing a vigor-based program can be difficult because this may mean not using a very good looking boar or sow that has shown up some breeding weakness. Such decisions are never easy, but providing your overall program is doing well, then such decisions must be made in the interests of long-term planning.

Strain Building

Commencing with good stock is only one of the many ingredients of success in breeding. Possibly the most important attribute a breeder can have is the ability to make good selective decisions about which stock to retain and which to sell. Although one hears people say that he or she has a natural eye for quality, it is probably more true to say that such an 'eye' comes from many years of observing what constitutes quality more than any inborn ability. It is therefore essential that a breeder studies the standard for his variety and becomes aware what the judges are looking for when interpreting the standard. Once one has built a strong mental image of what the ideal is likely to be, then one can seek to produce this in one's own stock by judicious selection for only the very best examples.

Having acquired one or two related boars, together with three to five sows, one can commence the long-term planning of matings. The acquisition of good boars is vital because the future strain will be built around their believed qualities. The boar is no more important in passing on virtues than is the sow, regardless of what you may be told to the contrary,

A golden agouti boar. The undercoat is ticked with red, producing a deep mahogany or chestnut color.

nor is the reverse true. The boar, however, is more influential on long-term breeding results because he has a far greater opportunity to spread his genes throughout your stock. Even if you decide to base your program from an especially superb sow, it is likely you will spread her genes via her best sons as this is the quickest way to instill her type into the rest of the stock being retained.

Once underway, your objective is to keep the introduction of outside stock to the very minimum because if this is not done then you will be continually introducing genes of which you have no historical knowledge on their relative purity.

Health Matters

The good stock person is someone who devotes all his attention to learning how to prevent illness rather than how to cure it! However, in order to do one, an understanding of the other is somewhat obligatory. It is quite surprising how each of us actually contributes, at least to some degree, in increasing the risk of illness in our stock in spite of all of our efforts to maintain good conditions in the stockroom. The rationale for this conclusion is rooted in the fact that, by housing a number of guinea pigs together, we automatically risk the spread of infection should one of our guineas become ill. We visit and exhibit our stock at shows where there are many cavies in a confined area, any one of which could be incubating an illness. We visit pet shops which may have ill guinea pigs and we visit the homes of fellow fanciers. On every occasion mentioned, we expose ourselves or our stock to the likelihood of airborne disease that we then transport back to our own stockrooms. These, of course, are normal everyday risks that must be taken if a hobby is to be followed, but, with this knowledge, we must make every effort to counter such risks by maintaining a constantly high standard of cleanliness in our stockroom.

Hutches must be cleaned at least every week and, if you have more than one guinea pig, you should ideally wash your hands after handling each one—and most certainly so whenever you suspect that one may be ill.

All floors, walls, and ceilings of stockrooms should be washed down periodically and repainted about every second year at least. All food should be subject to regular checks that it is not only clean but of a good nutritional quality—no bruised apples or overripe fruit or moldy vegetables. Feeding dishes should be washed daily and not just when they look decidedly unpresentable. Any cracked or chipped dishes should be replaced immediately.

Many problems can be averted simply by being aware of your stock on an individual basis. In this way, tell-tale signs may indicate things are not well; a normally greedy feeder may suddenly pick over its food, a lively guinea may sit hunched in the corner or not appear out of its bedding area. A slight chill may be noticed in one of the guineas whose eye may not be as sparkling as they should be, or the droppings seem abnormal. When you are unable to spend a little time studying each guinea pig you own, your stock is too large or you need some help with basic chores so you can spend more time with the guineas.

An unwell guinea pig is not difficult to spot because either its eyes, nose, motions, or fur will not be normal, it will normally go off its food or eat very little and will also be more lethargic than usual. The first thing to do is to isolate it and maintain a good temperature so that in its reduced state of health it does not compound matters by becoming chilled. Do not feed greenfoods but supply a dry cereal mix and, of course, water. If you are new to keeping guinea pigs, then you are advised to contact a veterinarian and describe the symptoms or, ensuring the guinea pig is placed in a secure box with plenty of fresh hay, take the animal to the vet's office.

A healthy guinea pig is bright-eyed, active, and alert.

What you must never do with guinea pigs (or rabbits) is attempt to supply antibiotics, should these be available from druggists as they are in certain countries. This is because the guinea pig has in its digestive system numerous beneficial bacteria that are vital to its digestion of food—these are destroyed by certain antibiotics, thus enabling harmful bacteria to develop. Antibiotics may destroy both gram-positive and gram-negative bacteria so must be administered strictly under supervision. It is for this reason that your vet will change the prescribed treatment after initial use of an antibiotic in order to reduce the risk of its actions upon beneficial organisms.

In the following text, the more common problems likely to be encountered are reviewed, but it must be stressed that many diseases have the same or similar initial clinical symptoms and often only microscopy will determine the exact cause of a disease. Home treatment may well cure minor ailments but the problem is that if it is not, in fact, a minor health matter then valuable time may have been lost in treatment. In general, if an unwell guinea pig has not showed obvious improvement to home treatment within 48 hours, you are advised to consult your veterinarian.

DIARRHEA

Diarrhea and enteritis are the direct results of other internal problems. These rarely have single causes unless in mild forms, resulting from too much greenfood, in which case its not being fed should rapidly clear up the problem. If diarrhea does not quickly clear, and if it is accompanied by other symptoms, such as weeping eyes, nose, or mouth, immediate veterinary help is required; certain complaints can be transmitted to humans so in all cases the washing of hands is essential after handling such a guinea pig. A few pairs of disposable medical gloves are useful for handling sick animals.

In all cases where any form of diarrhea has been seen, all bedding should be removed and burnt; the hutch should be thoroughly cleaned with a

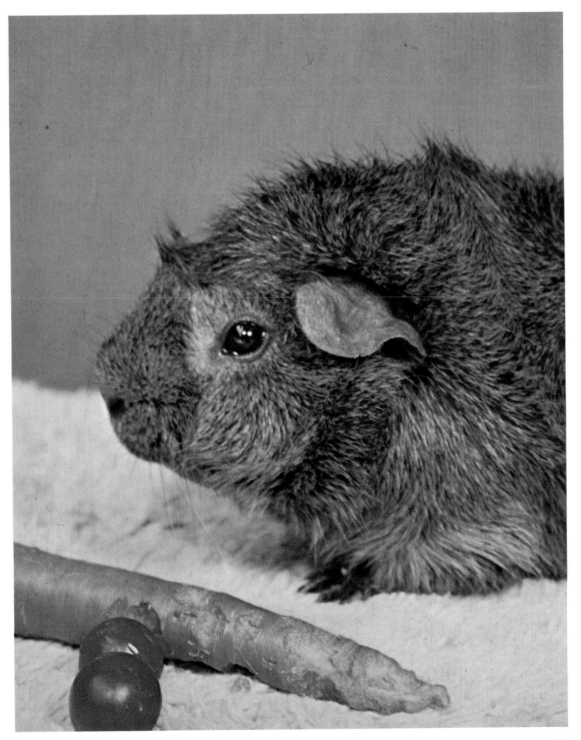

mild disinfectant and, ideally, allowed to remain empty for a few weeks, during which time it should receive further cleaning.

SKIN COMPLAINTS

Should you notice your guinea pig scratching a lot, inspect it carefully for signs of lice or mites. It can be stated that rodents are rarely affected by fleas—your cat or dog is more likely to have these than your guinea pig. Lice can be seen in the hair as tiny grayish slow moving creatures. Their eggs, known as nits, are often visible as elongated white specks clinging to the hairs. They have one dubious advantage which is that they complete their entire life cycle on the host so are far easier to eradicate than mites.

Treatment will be via a suitable acaracide from your pet shop or vet, and must be performed at least twice in order to kill off hatching eggs. Lice are transmitted by direct contact with another animal so both guinea pigs and other pets should be kept away from a guinea under treatment.

Mites are a different proposition because they invariably complete their lifecycles away from the host: in crevices of woodwork, under litter trays and in similar places. Treatment will be the same but here it is the home-base that is crucial to your success. Burn all bedding and ideally blowtorch the hutch and repaint with a suitably acaracide impregnated emulsion paint. Both lice and mites live by sucking the blood of their host, thus creating irritation. In severe cases, it is likely that anemia could set in—especially with young animals and, in such a weakened state, they are likely to succumb to secondary infection.

Balding patches are usually a clear indication of mites, which can be introduced to singly kept pets via bedding or by other means including your other pets.

Another particularly difficult skin problem is known as ringworm. It is not actually a worm at all but a fungal infection in which you will see circular type bald patches on the skin; scurf and crust-like scabs will also form. Veterinary treatment will cure the problem but

Opposite: **Kids and cavies can become great friends. As with any kind of pet, children should be taught how to properly handle the animal.**

single treatment is rarely successful because the fungal spores can live quite a long time away from the host—in hutches, bedding, almost anywhere. Your vet will be able to provide you with a special disinfectant to counter further fungal growths. Once again the hutch should be subjected to the flame of a blowtorch— but beware you do not set fire to your pet's house!

A most useful aid to have when dealing with external parasites is a good hand-held magnifying glass so that you can carefully check the condition of your stock's skin on a regular basis.

WORMS

Guinea pigs can be affected by both roundworm and tapeworms, and while the incidence is low, keep an eye on the feces for the tiny white tell-tale signs of worms. In fact, most animals have worms of some sort or another, a number of which are quite harmless and live within the digestive systems. However, in the case of some species, they create problems if in high numbers because they deprive the animal of nutrition and generally debilitate it. Further, they may be the cause of bacterial introduction to the animal.

Worms can be transmitted via the feces of dogs or cats onto greenfood, such as grass, which is why care should be exercised when gathering this and why it must always be washed carefully **before being fed** to your pets. Treatment can be any of the popular wormifuges available from either your pet shop or veterinarian. Worms can be passed from a sow to her offspring indicating why some breeders choose to worm sows shortly before they are due to have a litter, but this is not essential. A very good preventive tonic for many animals is to mix either cloves of garlic or liquid garlic into their mash—not too much. This is a time-proven remedy against worms and many other problems.

CLAW TRIMMING

If claws become overgrown, they should be trimmed back to a suitable length, being careful not to cut too deeply and hitting the blood supply—this is easily seen in light or non-

An adorable pair of long-coated guinea pigs. To some people, the guinea pig is unsurpassed as a lovable, gentle little pet.

pigmented claws, but less so in dark ones, in which case do not trim as much off.

STRESS

There is no doubt that stress contributes considerably to inducing a great many ailments in the guinea pig, which is by nature a rather nervous little animal. Stress is mental fear, whether real or imagined; it consumes energy and, in so doing, reduces the guinea pig's ability to fight off disease. It can be created simply by moving a pet from one location to the next, by sudden noises, by any major changes in the guinea pig's environment, or by a sow being split up from other cavies with which she has been living. Mice and especially rats will frighten a guinea pig, so this is a factor of which you must always beware and try to take into account.

It can be seen that in nearly all cases of disease or minor ailments the common link is cleanliness, good food, and sound accommodation. If these are given constant attention then you will be unfortunate indeed to ever have more than acceptable levels of minor ailments to cope with, but, remember, always be ever vigilant!

Index

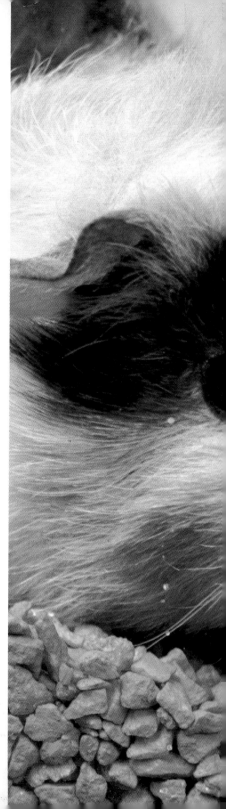